Robert Pace

EACHING AIDS

Key Signatures

U.S. $5.95

HL00372118

Distributed by
HAL LEONARD PUBLISHING CORPORATION
7777 West Bluemound Road P.O. Box 13819 Milwaukee, WI 53213

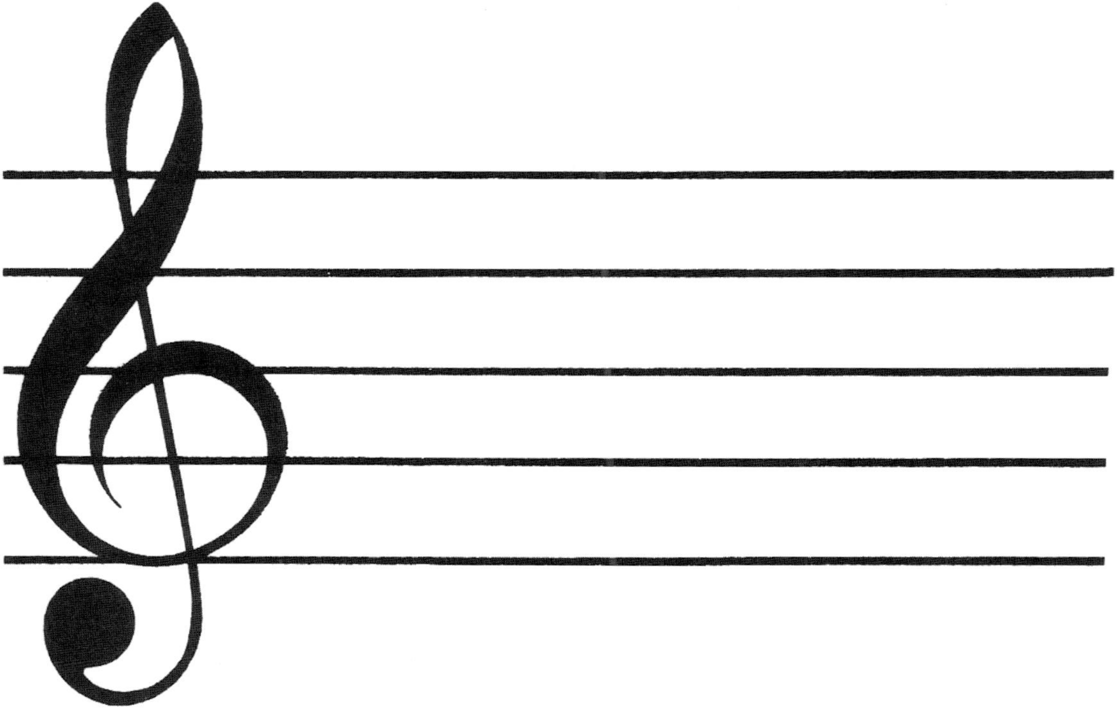

C Major

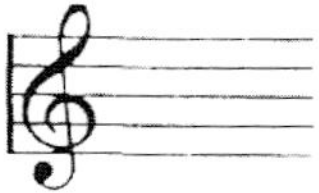

A Minor

LEE ROBERTS MUSIC PUBLICATIONS, INC.

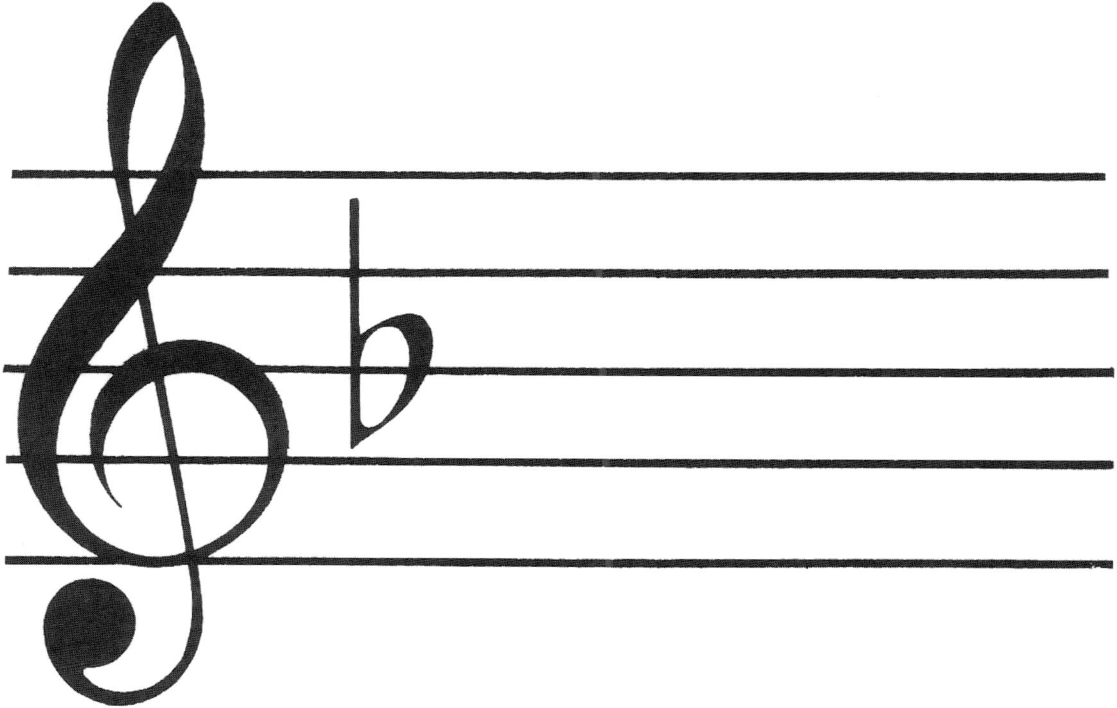

F Major

D Minor

LEE ROBERTS MUSIC PUBLICATIONS, INC

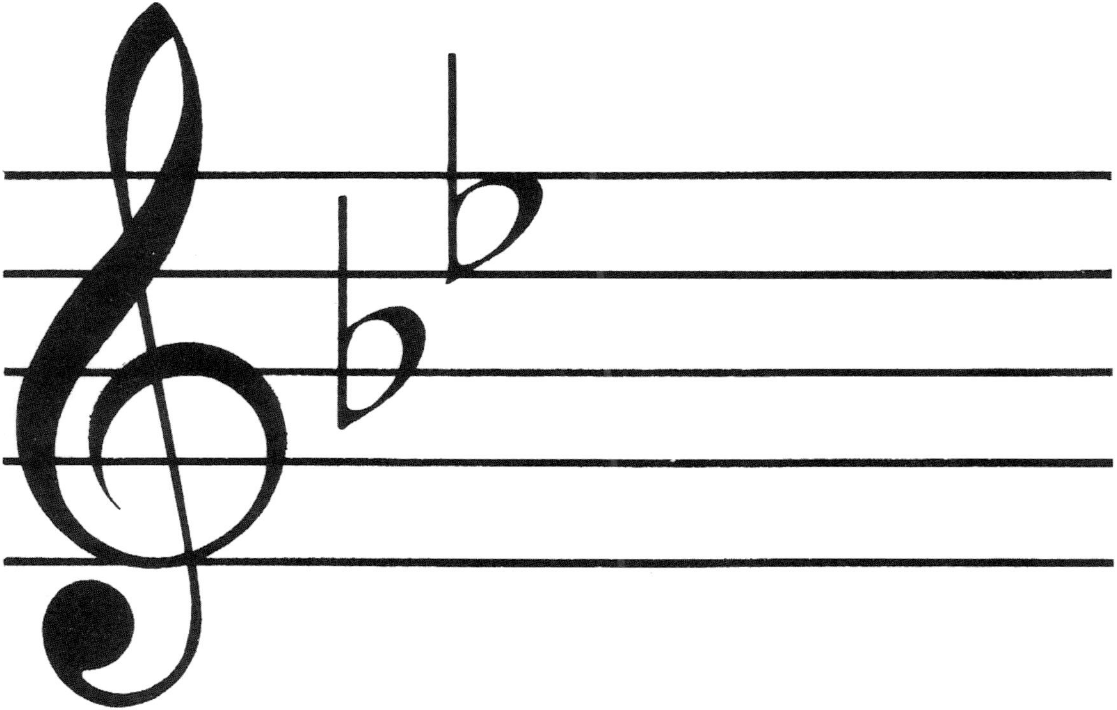

B♭ Major

G Minor

LEE ROBERTS MUSIC PUBLICATIONS, INC.,

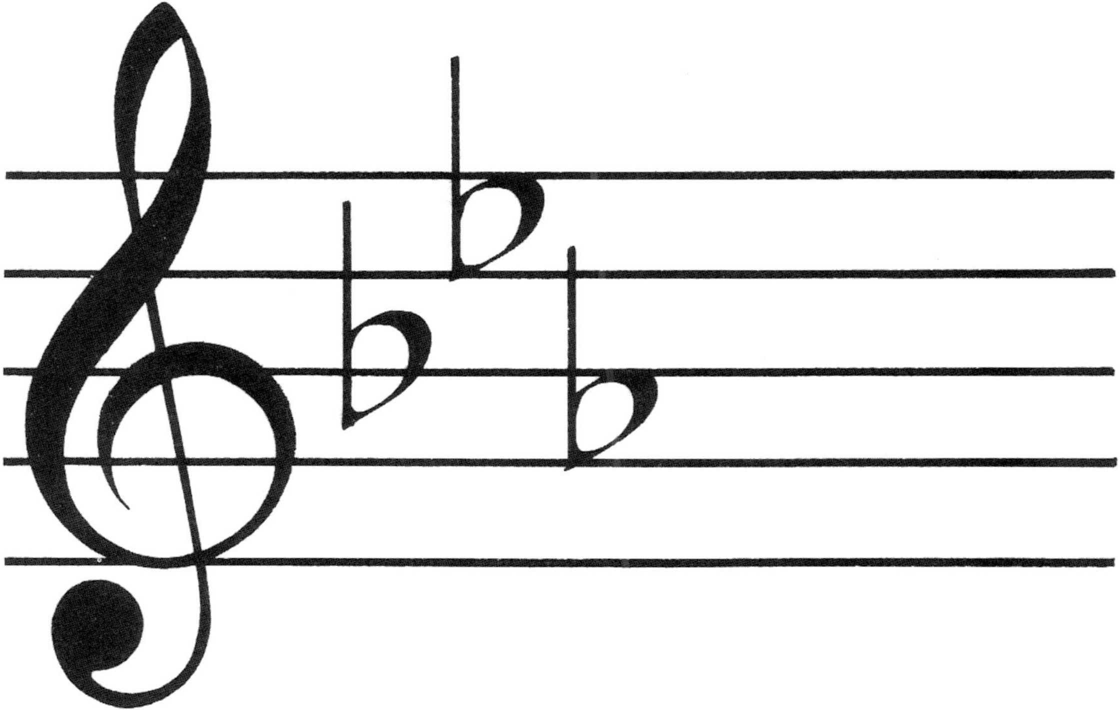

E♭ Major

C Minor

LEE ROBERTS MUSIC PUBLICATIONS, INC.

A♭ Major

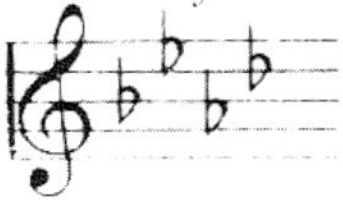

F Minor

LEE ROBERTS MUSIC PUBLICATIONS, INC.

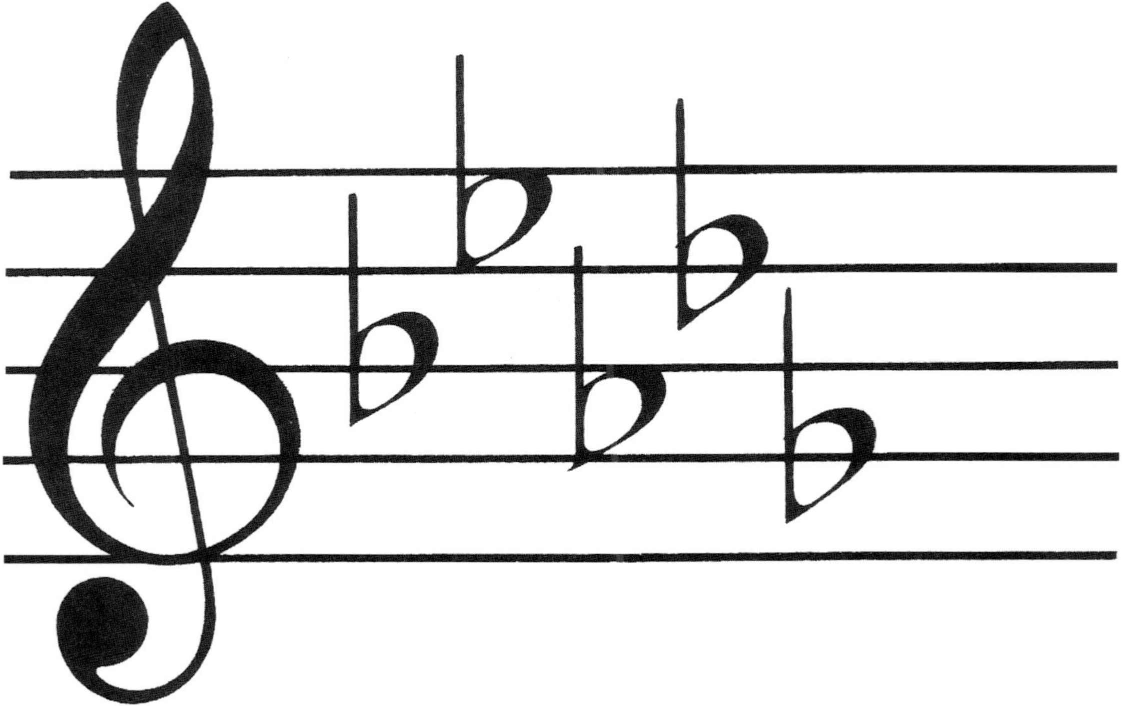

D♭ Major

B♭ Minor

LEE ROBERTS MUSIC PUBLICATIONS, INC.

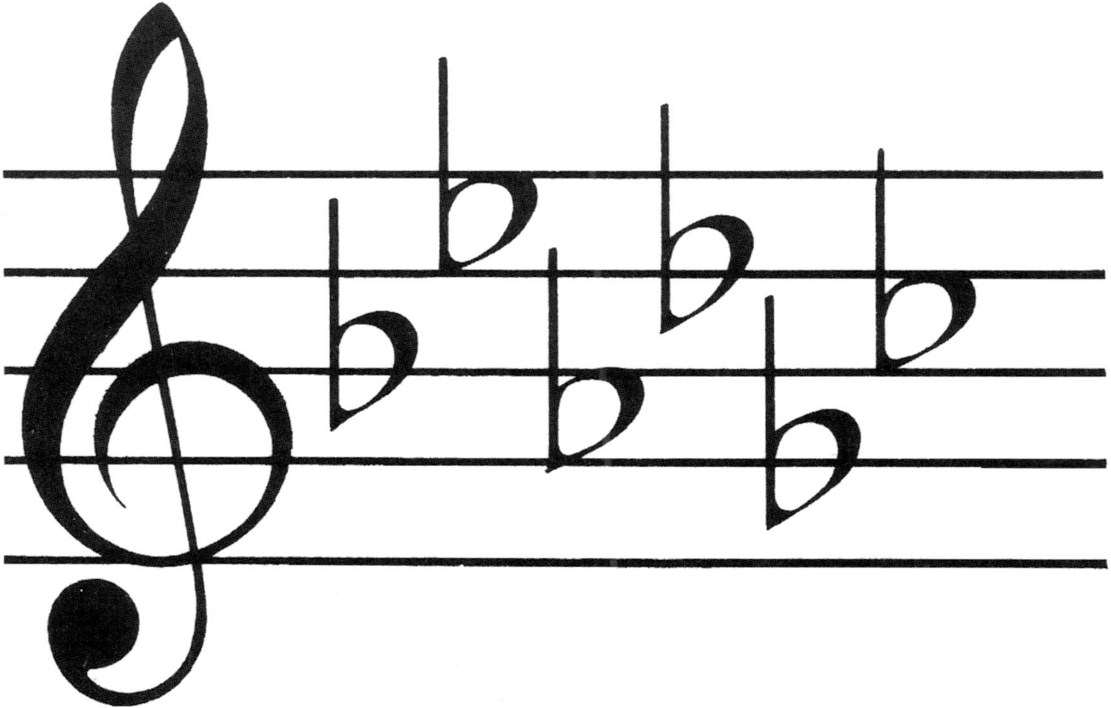

G♭ Major

E♭ Minor

LEE ROBERTS MUSIC PUBLICATIONS, INC.

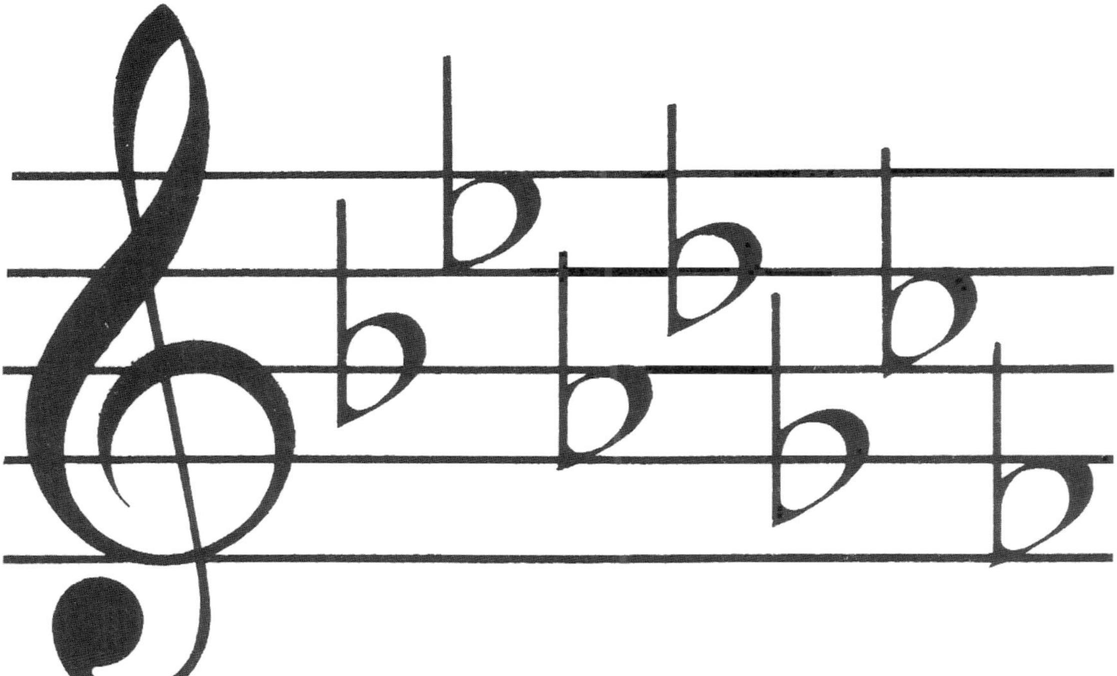

C♭ Major

A♭ Minor

LEE ROBERTS MUSIC PUBLICATIONS, INC.

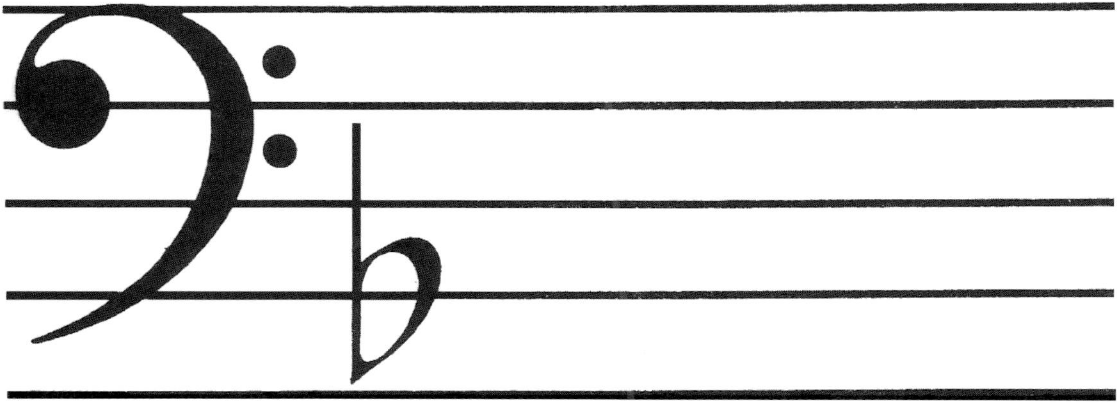

F Major

D Minor

LEE ROBERTS MUSIC PUBLICATIONS, INC.

C Major

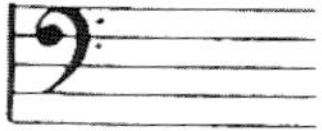

A Minor

LEE ROBERTS MUSIC PUBLICATIONS, INC.

B♭ Major

G Minor

LEE ROBERTS MUSIC PUBLICATIONS, INC.

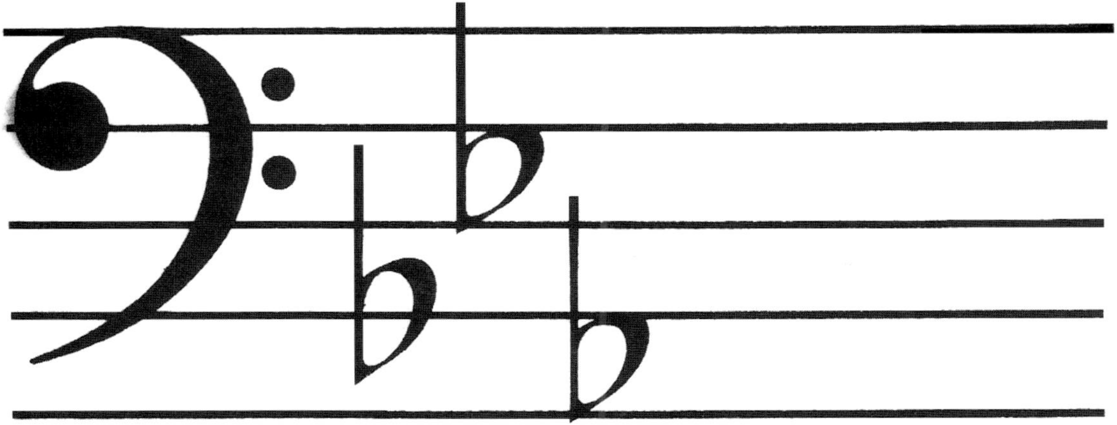

E♭Major

C Minor

LEE ROBERTS MUSIC PUBLICATIONS, INC.

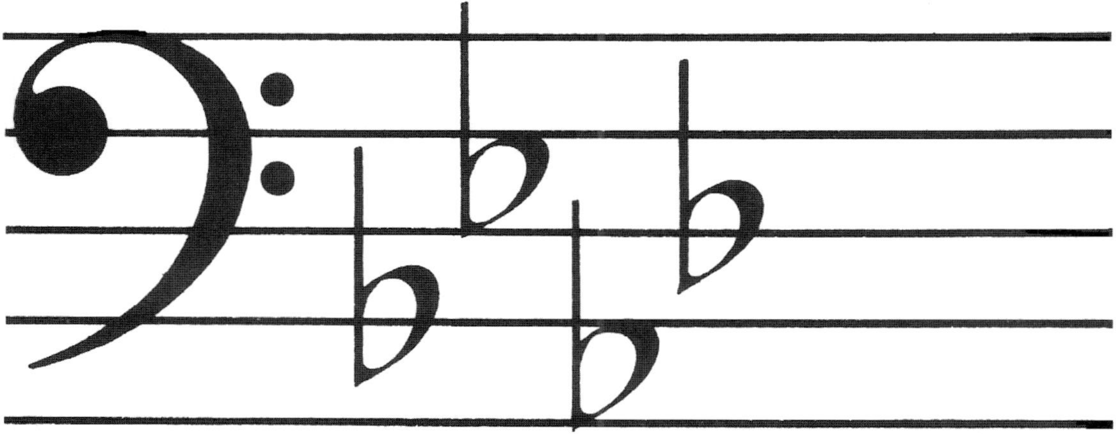

A♭ Major

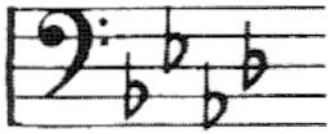

F Minor

LEE ROBERTS MUSIC PUBLICATIONS, INC.

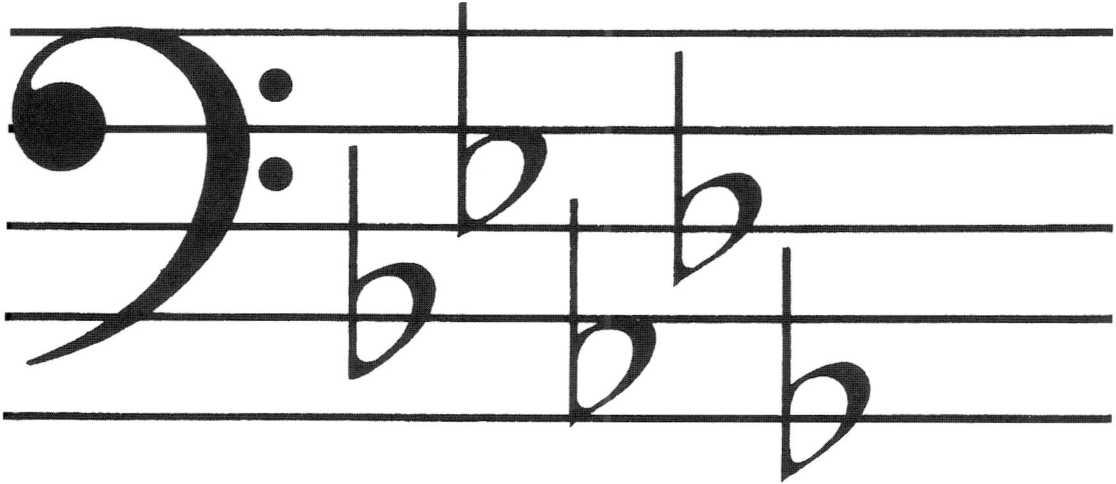

D♭ Major

B♭ Minor

LEE ROBERTS MUSIC PUBLICATIONS, INC.

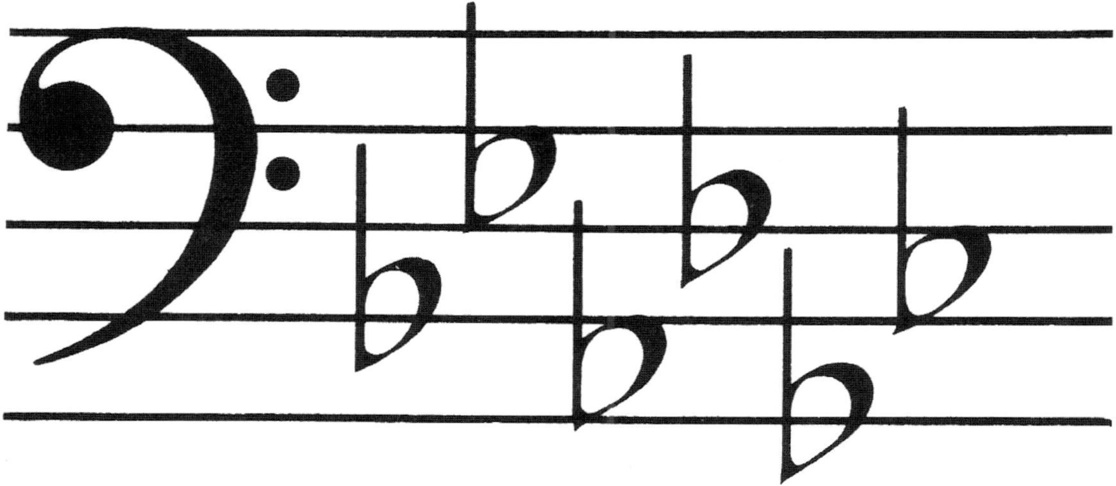

G♭ Major

E♭ Minor

LEE ROBERTS MUSIC PUBLICATIONS, INC.

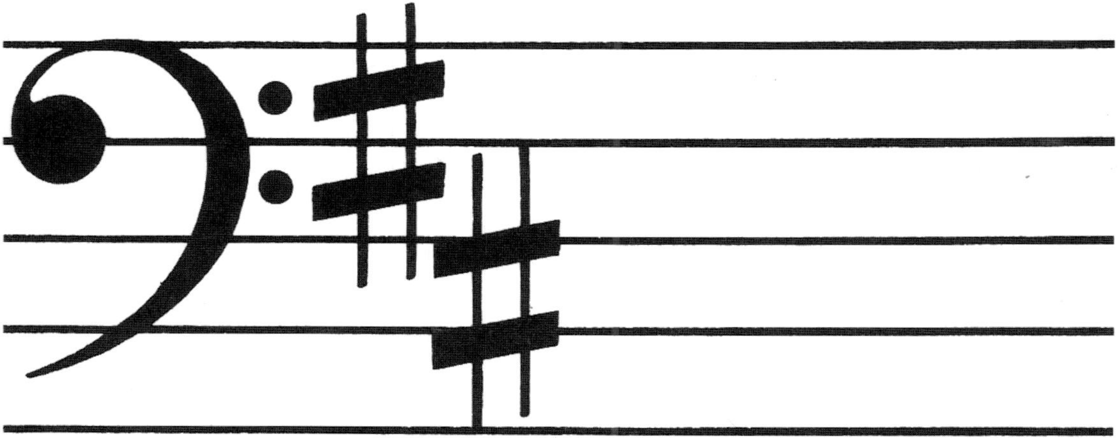

D Major

B Minor

LEE ROBERTS MUSIC PUBLICATIONS, INC.

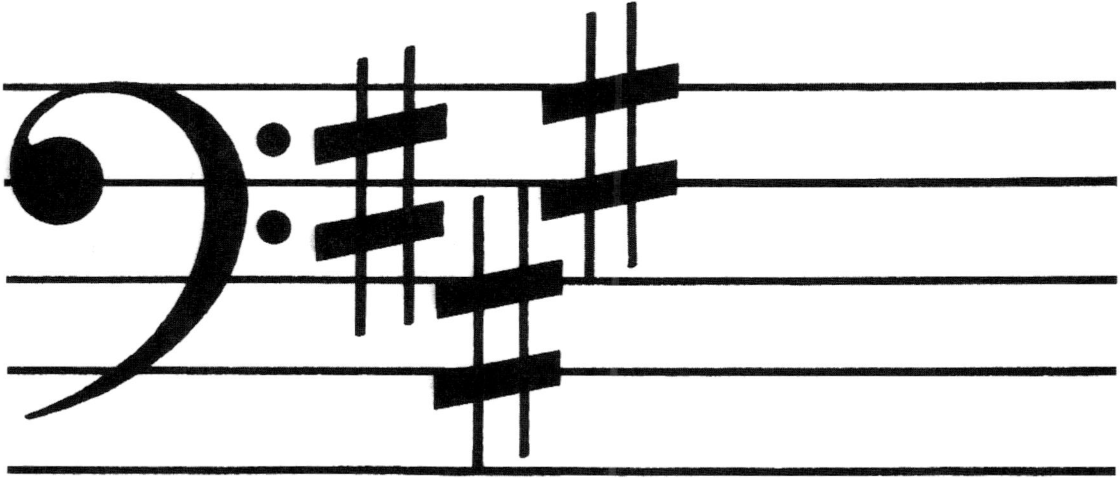

A Major

F♯ Minor

LEE ROBERTS MUSIC PUBLICATIONS, INC.

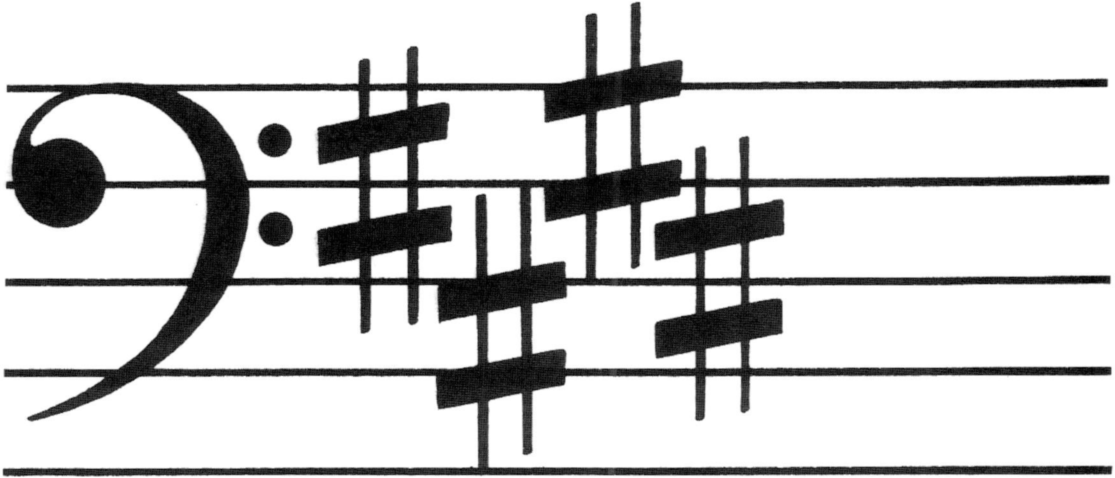

E Major

C♯ Minor

LEE ROBERTS MUSIC PUBLICATIONS, INC.

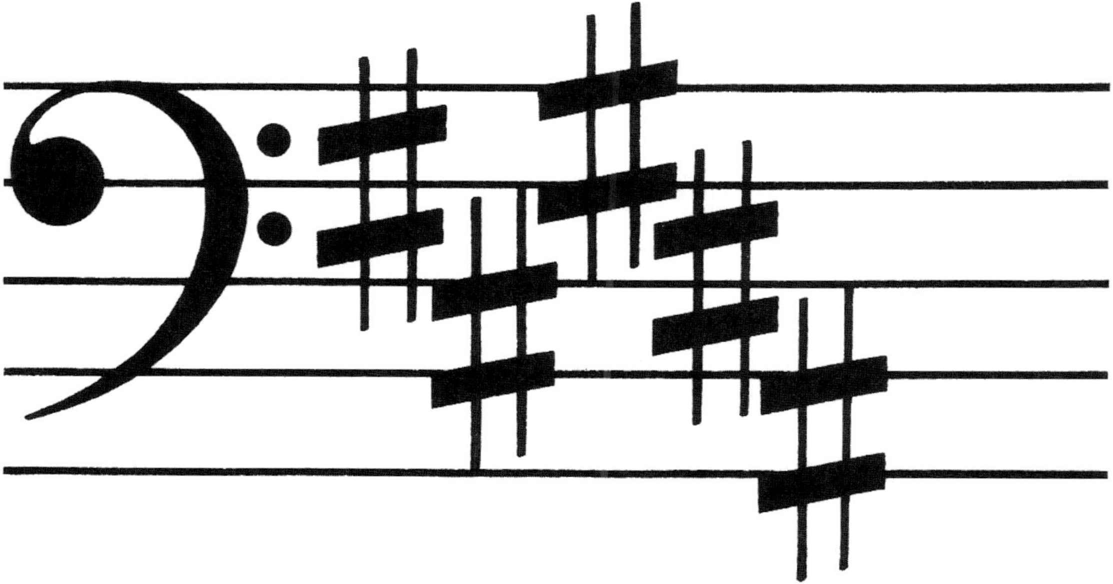

B Major

G# Minor

LEE ROBERTS MUSIC PUBLICATIONS, INC.

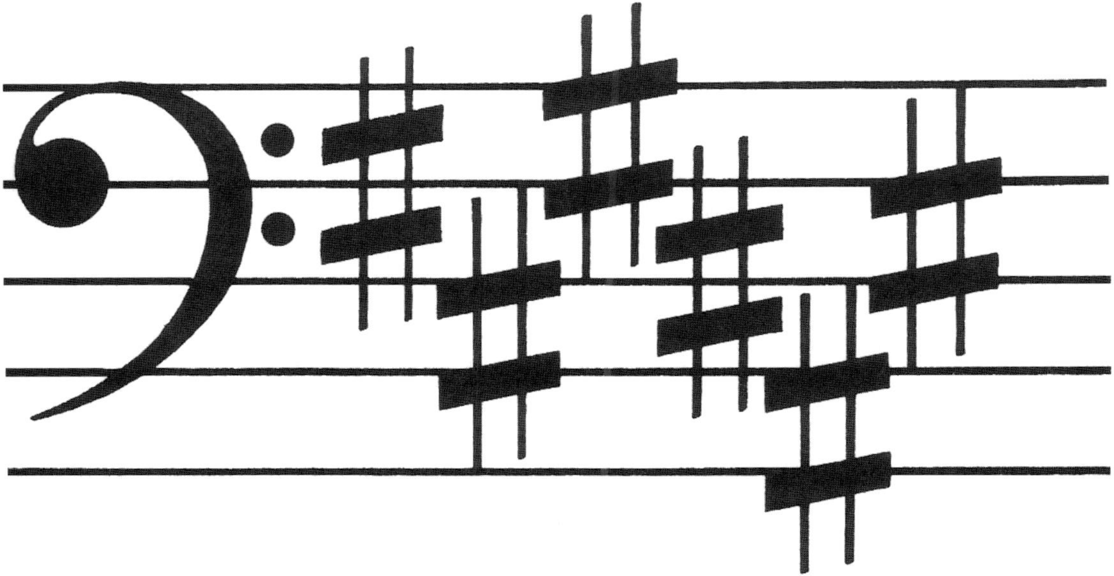

F♯ Major

D♯ Minor

LEE ROBERTS MUSIC PUBLICATIONS, INC.

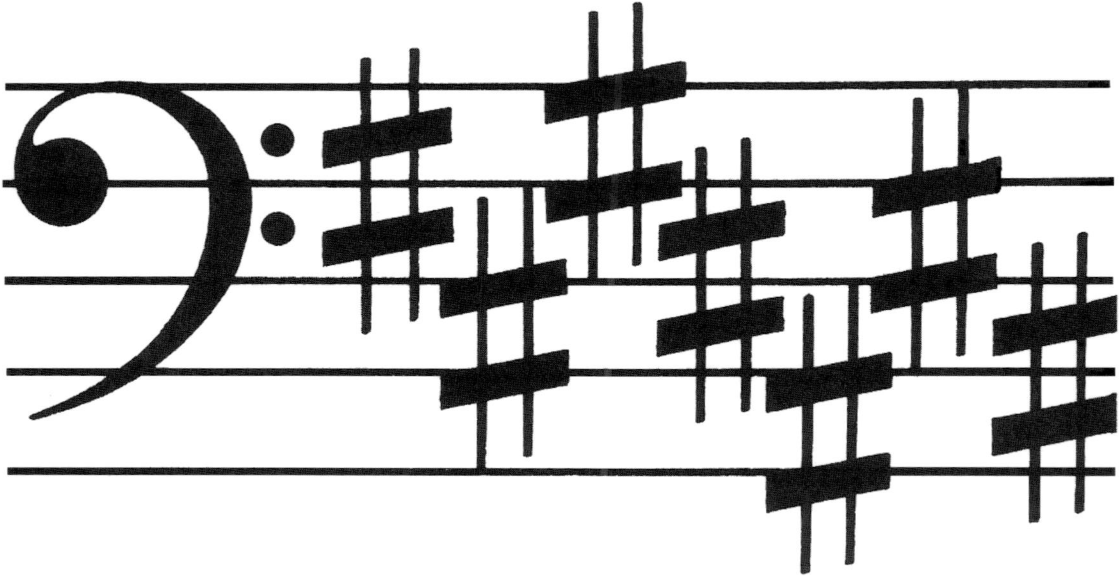

C♯ Major

A♯ Minor

LEE ROBERTS MUSIC PUBLICATIONS, INC.

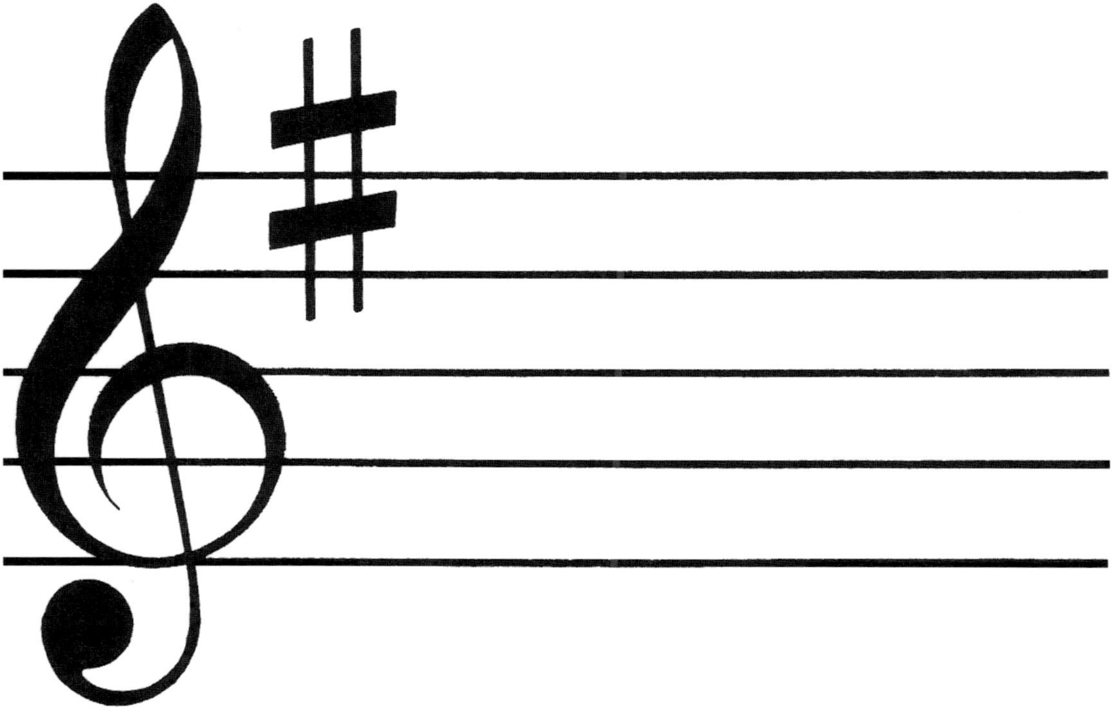

G Major

E Minor

LEE ROBERTS MUSIC PUBLICATIONS, INC.

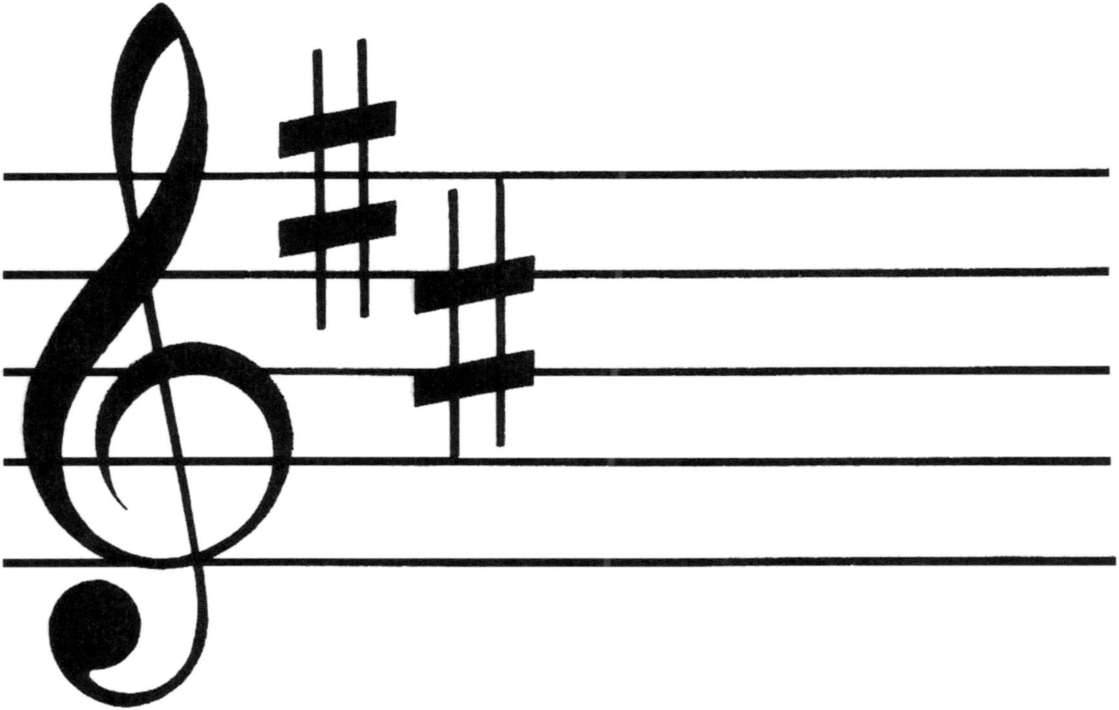

D Major

B Minor

LEE ROBERTS MUSIC PUBLICATIONS, INC.

A Major

F♯ Minor

LEE ROBERTS MUSIC PUBLICATIONS, INC.

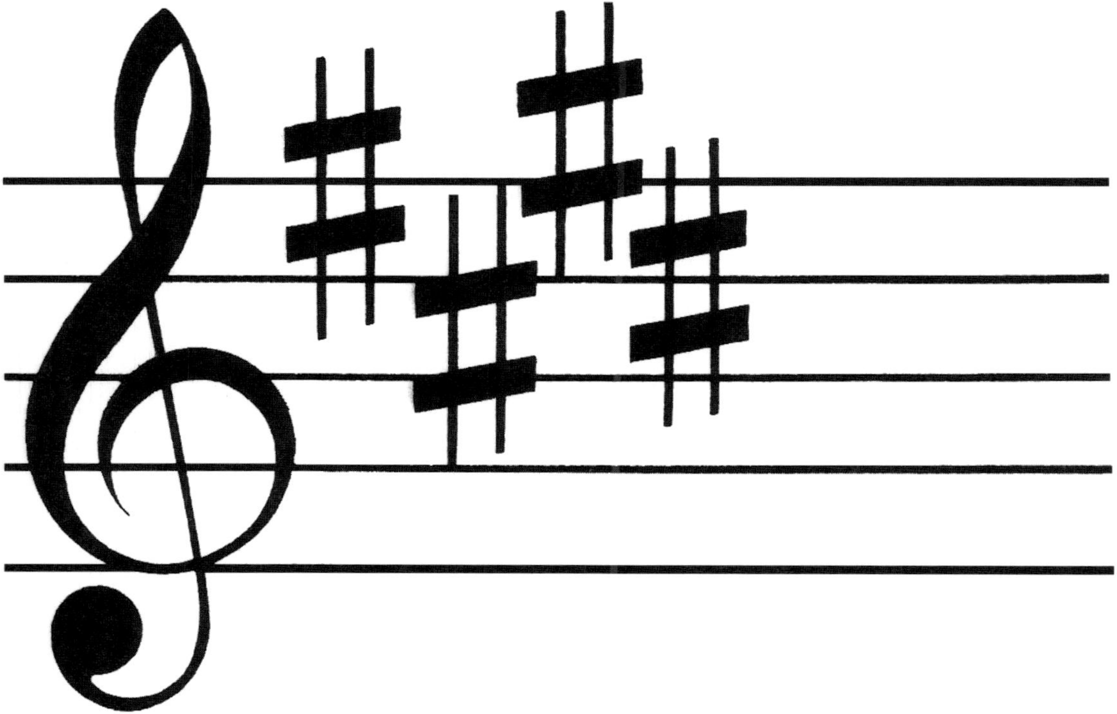

E Major

C♯ Minor

LEE ROBERTS MUSIC PUBLICATIONS, INC.

B Major

G♯ Minor

LEE ROBERTS MUSIC PUBLICATIONS, INC.

F♯ Major

D♯ Minor

LEE ROBERTS MUSIC PUBLICATIONS, INC.

G Major

E Minor

LEE ROBERTS MUSIC PUBLICATIONS, INC.

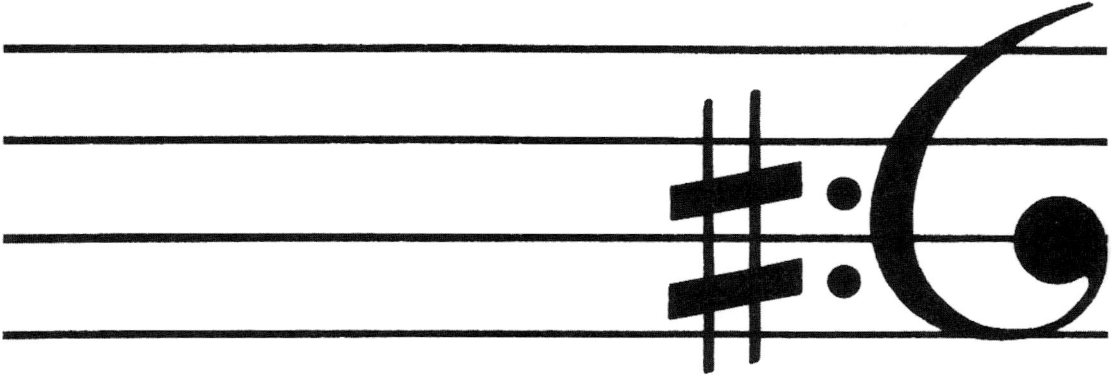

C♭ Major

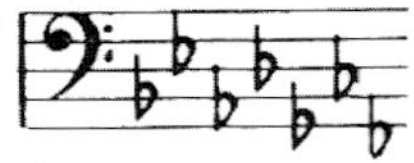

A♭ Minor

LEE ROBERTS MUSIC PUBLICATIONS, INC.

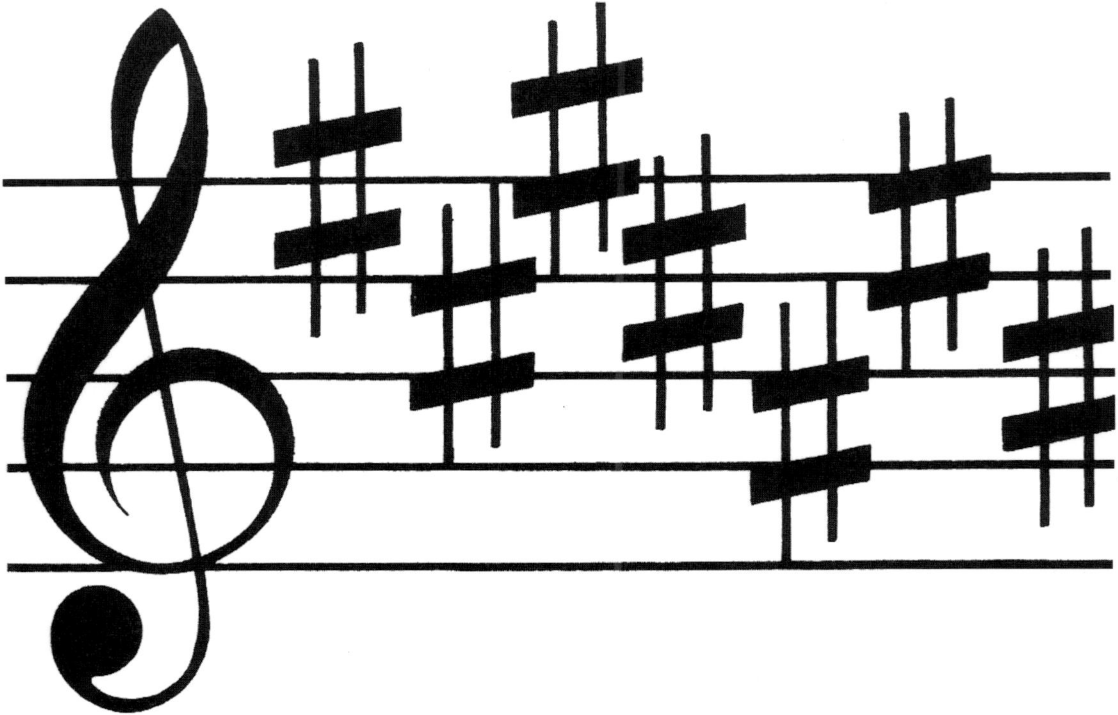

C# Major

A# Minor

ISBN 0-7935-2904-2

LEE ROBERTS MUSIC PUBLICATIONS, INC.,